I Thought I Had Something to Say
2014 Facebook Posts by Stephanie Mott

What would inspire a person to believe that their Facebook posts should be assembled into a book? I think it has more to do with capturing some of the things I have said, than it does with believing that there is anything special about them.

At any rate, as a transgender woman and civil rights activist, I believe that it is important to see someone who is transgender as more than just someone who is transgender. I have thoughts and feelings, hopes and dreams, purpose and values.

A very good and well-respected man was once talking publicly about values, and after his talk, I went to him and told him that I also have values. He said to me, "I hope so."

This man, who was in a position of considerable power, had determined my character by the fact that I am transgender.

So, I guess that it's important for me to be as open about my values as I am about being transgender. Perhaps, it will help make a difference in how people see people who happen to be transgender. I hope so.

For My Moms!

ISBN: 978-1-312-80673-3

I Thought I Had Something to Say
2014 Facebook Posts by Stephanie Mott

~ December 31, 2014

Having been properly inspired and mentored by Mr. Kitty, I shall endeavor to do honor to his expertise by taking a nap.

~ December 30, 2014

My hope is that by being openly-transgender, people will see our truths more clearly. How sad that any young person would not be able to believe they can be their authentic self. My heart is broken but my resolve is re-doubled again.

~ December 28, 2014

All the struggling became my greatest gift at the very moment I realized I had been prepared to help another human being.

One of the bumper stickers on my car.

~ December 25, 2014

My Christmas of 2005

In November 2005, I became a guest of the Topeka Rescue Mission (TRM). I was 3 days sober and still trying to live as a man, although I had finally made the decision to do what I needed to do to be okay. I was 47 years old and living as a man was clearly not working for me; clearly not ever going to work for me.

TRM was not the place in 2005 for me to come out as transgender. It was a warm place and they fed me. For my stay I had the chore and the honor of sweeping the floor at the TRM store on North Kansas Avenue. It was the first thing I took pride in doing in a very long time, and it helped to begin to fill the giant spiritual hole that my soul had become.

I would spend my first Thanksgiving in sobriety at the mission and on the last day of 2005, I spent my 48th birthday there. In between, was the Christmas of 2005.

At 47 days sober, the sickness of detoxification had mostly subsided and my mind was more clear than it had been in a long time. I had been approved for admission into the Valeo drug and alcohol inpatient program about two weeks later and I was

2

feeling very grateful that I wasn't spending my Christmas living under a bridge.

We got to pick out two Christmas gifts from a table full of necessities and I chose a warm pair of socks and a pair of gloves. I was very happy to have them. Humiliation had begun to become some degree of humility and I was thinking that maybe it was possible that things could work out for me if I did what I needed to do (although I had no real clue at the time what that looked like).

We had a great and wonderful meal in the cafeteria that day; a traditional Christmas dinner. I will forever remember the slice of pumpkin pie I enjoyed and the warm and friendly smiles of the volunteers who were serving us. This was a day that another spark of hope became part of my soul.

Nine years later, my life has changed more than I could have possibly imagined. Right this moment, I am exceedingly glad that my life has not changed so much that I wouldn't remember my Christmas of 2005.

Much has changed since Christmas of 2005

~ December 24, 2014

I do believe in Santa. I do. It's true. I never stopped believing.

I don't know about a magical man in a red suit and flying reindeer and all that stuff, but I believe in the everywhere, all around the globe part.

I don't think it's something that happens only on Christmas eve or Christmas day or on any particular day. Maybe it happens each and every day, if we only have enough faith to believe in the power of one person caring enough to give freely for no other purpose than to lift another person's spirit.

I don't know the name it goes by, I think maybe different names for different people. I think a lot of people would say that it is often recognizable as love or random acts of kindness or devotion in the face of turmoil.

Maybe it is that something that gives us hope when there is no perceivable reason to have hope. The light in the darkness. The strength in the face of fear. The invisible force that stirs a person to put one foot in front of the other no matter how hard the struggle is. The hand that comes from nowhere to reach out and let another soul know that they are not alone.

Oh yes, I do believe in Santa, but we don't have to call it Santa. We can just call it love.

~ December 24, 2014

Kindness is an artist. It creates images of hope.

~ December 23, 2014

Ours is such a wonderful, horrible, beautiful, harmful, uplifting, heartbreaking, comforting, stressful, peaceful, war-infested, loving, and hateful world. It's all very confusing. How does one make sense of it all?

I think, what it all means is this. I should do what I can to make the world more wonderful, less horrible, more beautiful, less harmful, more uplifting, less heartbreaking, more comforting, less stressful, more peaceful, less war-infested, more loving, and less hateful.

I'm not sure what else I need to know. And now, it makes perfect sense to me.

~ December 23, 2014

All that is ever asked of us is that we love each other.

~ December 22, 2014

I know the pain that is burned into the cries of people who are oppressed. I know the pain of the soul-crushing air when you are considered to be a lesser human being. That air is in every breath I take. It participates in every thought that enters my mind and influences every choice I make. I choose not to compare one oppression to another. I choose to dedicate myself to the elimination of all oppression. I made this choice yesterday. I make this choice today. I will make this choice tomorrow. No one should ever be considered to be less than. I can not sit silently in a world that continues, far too often, to turn its eyes away from the needless suffering we inflict on each other. My heartache must be matched by my voice and my feet, or my soul will surely die.

~ December 21, 2014

Love is the spoon that stirs the soup in a different direction.

~ December 21, 2014

Being radical doesn't mean you separate yourself from love. If there is something more radical than unconditional love, I don't know what it is. What could be more radical than giving with no interest or intention of gaining?

~ December 21, 2014

I know there is hope for the world. I see it every time one person gives freely to another.

~ December 20, 2014

Violence is never the answer to violence. My heart mourns from the tragedies of our world. All of them. My heart yearns for the conversations that must take place before the violence can come to an end.

Lillian Irene (Calvin) Mott
April 12, 1928 - December 18, 1989

"I can only imagine what my birth mom would have thought about Stephanie. But I imagine she would have been thrilled and proud. She only wanted one thing for me and that was for me to be happy."

~ December 19, 2014

When I think about what I would like to do in this world, and where I would like to go, I also think about what I need to be able to do those things and go to those places.

I need faith. Not necessarily faith in a greater being, but faith in a greater good. Faith that my journey is making a difference. Faith that there is something better out there waiting for someone to dare to dream, to discover, to do.

Faith that the first step will lead to the next step. Faith that I am neither so special, nor not special enough, that I can't be one who dares to dream, and discover, and do.

I need perspective. More than understanding that my journey is making a difference, it is a gift to understand that even if I don't reach the so-called end of the journey, I have given others hope along the way. I have broken or defeated or bumped or perhaps only shined light on the barriers along the way. And in breaking or defeating or bumping or shining light on those barriers, I have made the journey more achievable for the next person who is following in my footsteps. Even as the footsteps of those who have gone before me have been my guide, and my strength, and my inspiration. Ever knowing that the journey of those yet to come will undoubtedly take them to places of which I have not the vision to see.

I need compassion. The roads of the journey are marvelously interconnected and the hearts I lift up will become the means by which I am able to reach higher than I ever dreamed possible. While the hearts I tear down will be like anchors on my soul, keeping me from even being able to dream.

Whatever else I may need will surely be delivered if I have faith, perspective, and compassion. Whatever else I need will come from the air I breathe. It will come from the light that shines or the storms that fury. It will come from friends and enemies and strangers. It will come from the essence of life contained in the choosing to dare to dream, and discover, and do.

~ December 19, 2014

True beauty is a quality of the soul. Beauty is a random act of kindness, two people in love, the way a dog reacts when their human comes home. Beauty is one of the ways I can treat others. If I want to be beautiful, I should do beautiful.

~ December 17, 2014

*25 years ago, right now, my father, together with
my brothers and sisters and me, were making the
decision to have the doctors stop intervening in the
progression of my mother's battle with pancreatic
cancer. Several hours later, she would take her
last breath (December 18, 1989).*

*I am among the blessed children who have had two
moms. I guess my version of having two moms is
not the traditional way - the traditional way to
have two moms is to have them both at the same
time - I think.*

*My second mom came along back in 2007 and
gives me the amazing part of my journey in which I
get to be a daughter to her.*

*I can only imagine what my birth mom would have
thought about Stephanie. But I imagine she would
have been thrilled and proud. She only wanted one
thing for me and that was for me to be happy.*

*She is clearly responsible for a lot of the way I see
the world today. When I tell my story, I talk about
how she is the basis for anything I know about
unconditional love. It was a way of life for her.
Whatever part of my heart that seeks to love
unconditionally, that's the part where she still
lives.*

~ December 15, 2014

Sometimes people tell me that they think the things I do are courageous. I don't know. Maybe a little. But do you know what was truly courageous? Putting one foot in front of the other day after day after year after year, trying to be the person I thought I had to be, and waking up in the morning and deciding to breathe again, just for one more day. That was courage. This is pie.

Somewhere out there, someone is displaying courage far beyond what it takes to do the things I do today. They don't need me to be courageous. They need me to show them about pie. Easy as that.

~ December 14, 2014

I know today that not only can I survive, I can thrive, I can steer my ship into the storm, and look my fear in the eyes, and when I come out on the other side, nothing will be able to stop me from soaring into the sky.

~ December 12, 2014

What I didn't know, when things were the darkest for me, was that the storms and pain and fear and hopelessness were blowing and feeling and chasing and driving me to a place where I would have more to give than I ever thought possible. What I didn't know, was that this was the place I had been searching for, the place I needed to be, to find peace in my soul.

~ December 11, 2014

The capacity of the human heart to love is the most significant, wonderful, miraculous part of all existence. There is no force so powerful, no presence so encompassing, and no concept so enduring as to perform a simple act of random kindness, to show compassion for those who have harmed you, and to give of yourself for another's hope.

~ December 11, 2014

Wouldn't it be interesting if God turned out to be Whoopi Goldberg?

In December 2014, I began using two cameras to create views from different angles when recording the songs I have written. These photos were captured from the recordings. My songs can be found on YouTube.

~ December 6, 2014

I was raised as a boy. Seen as a boy. Taught to believe I could become anything I wanted to be. In the meantime, my dad told my sister that she didn't need to learn math because she was just going to be a housewife.

I was aware of male privilege. I thought I was good about not taking advantage of that privilege. Then, as I embraced my female self, and I began to be seen as a woman, I watched the perceived value of my opinion become less before my very eyes.

I began to understand that I had been taking advantage of my privilege all along. I realized that would always be true unless I actively worked to eliminate said privilege.

This is also true of my white privilege. I can fool myself into believing that I don't take advantage of being white. That can never be true unless I work to eliminate white privilege.

It can be difficult for me to see my white privilege from my own personal perspective. This is where dialogue comes into play. I must learn from other people who have different perspectives. I must put significant effort into seeing through the eyes of others; and embracing the knowledge of their lives and experiences.

I must work toward the day when all people have equitable opportunity. I can't take mine, at the expense of someone else. That's not the reason we are here. The reason we are here is to walk together toward a better world for everyone.

~ December 6, 2014

Fear can cause me to stand silent. Fear can turn my head so that I can not see. Fear can stop me from doing so many amazing things.

Fear can motivate me to speak out. Fear can allow me to look at the things I don't want to see. Fear can inspire me to do amazing things.

There is nothing wrong with being afraid. I need to  *recognize the call to action that is hidden in the shadows of fear, and shine the light on what can be done, instead of what can't be done.*

When the fear of leaving things the same becomes greater than the fear of changing them, all things are possible.

~ November 29, 2014

Let us sit down together, you and I, and talk to each other. Tell me your story so that I might better understand the obstacles you face because of the color of your skin. Listen to me as I share my journey as a transgender woman. Teach me how it feels to be Muslim in a Christian country. Share with me what it means to be blind, or deaf, or unable to walk. Help me know how you feel when they say you are too young to understand or too old to be relevant. Take me with you through poverty, or mental illness, or domestic violence, or sexual assault, or cancer. Let us find strength together and help each other and discover the power of unity and unconditional love.

~ November 28, 2014

The faces of oppression are many. Unity against oppression is born in our willingness to help fight the things that oppress others, in addition to the things that oppress our own.

~ November 27, 2014

While the meaning of Thanksgiving has changed for me since last year - I have become so much

*more aware of my own privilege - I have so much
to be thankful for.*

*So many wonderful friends have shown so much
amazing love in the last 12 days since my heart
attack. I haven't taken a breath in a very long time
when I did not feel the same love. I am honored to
walk on a justice road with each of you.*

*I am perhaps most thankful for the opportunity to
walk that road and try to help create a better
tomorrow. I am hoping and praying that the spirit
of thankfulness will find a home in all of our hearts
and strike a spark to light a fire of compassion and
love for all humankind.*

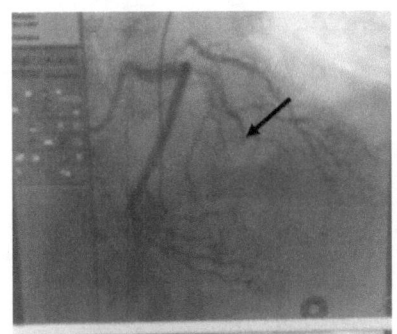
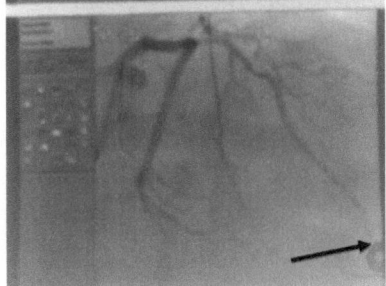

On November 15, I experienced a mild heart attack. These two pictures of my heart show where the blood flow was blocked (top) before the angioplasty and stents and the increased blood flow now.

The good news is that I got to the hospital before there was any significant damage, and I am doing very well.

~ November 25, 2014

And my soul is aching. For no matter 5 or 20 or 100 or 1000 people who climb from the wretches of oppression and carve spaces of their own in a granite world, far too many are born and live and die in a place where they never have a chance.

And my heart is breaking. For the days and months and years spent trying to offer hope, trying to bring about change, working to get people to see, could have been used to feed the hungry, create an army of Malalas, discover cures for disease.

And my mind is crying. For the multitude of sins, using power and wealth to oppress the oppressed, to deny the denied, to trod on the downtrodden, as wealth builds upon wealth, power solidifies power, and truth is defined by the words of their corporately-owned media.

And my hope is dying. For the endless invasion of those who have been led to believe that none of this is happening, not happening to them, even as it happens to each of us, until it has happened to all of us.

Then I take my dying hope and my crying mind and my breaking heart and my aching soul and I stand up. I will not be silent, I will not stop trying. I will not become as those who find their own self-worth by stomping on those who are down. Desperately trying to be less down than my neighbor of a different race, a different sexual orientation, a different ability, a different anything.

I will shine the light of love, respond not in kind but with kindness, teach forgiveness mixed with action, and fear more the idea of leaving things the way they are than I fear the idea of changing them.

~ November 24, 2014

Until we address the issues of racial profiling, overt acts of racism in society and within our own government, and the many tentacles of institutional racism in our country; until we examine why the law sees a white man with a gun differently than a black man with (or without) a gun; until we sit down together and honestly face our prejudices and fears; we will continue to watch young black men die needlessly.

~ November 23, 2014

I have this weird idea that everyone should have an equal chance. And this other weird idea that it's my responsibility to help make that happen.

~ November 22, 2014

Grace received is a builder of hope. Grace granted is a builder of character and a teacher of change.

~ November 13, 2014

I got to say "Congratulations" to some amazing people today. People who love each other. People who had the courage to walk into public spaces and declare their love out loud. People who walked in places they never dreamed of walking in their lifetime. People for whom discrimination seemed momentarily vanquished. People who stood up as definably equal human beings. #loveislove

~ November 12, 2014

There are tears in my eyes. Tears of joy. This is an historic day in Kansas. Much work to be done, but our love has been undeniably, irrefutably validated.

~ November 11, 2014

I'm too busy working on what might be to worry about what might have been.

~ November 11, 2014

They say freedom isn't free and I believe that.
Great Uncle Glenn stormed the beach at
Normandy. Grandpa Calvin served in World War
I. The gas he was exposed to undoubtedly
shortened his life. I was not quite three years old
when he died.

I am forever indebted to the women and men who
have fought for our freedom, and to those who still
do.

I am also forever indebted to the people who have
fought for the freedom of people who are
oppressed because of sexual orientation and
gender identity, and to those who still do.

May there come a day when both of these fights
are no longer necessary. In my own small way,
may I be part of the reason why that happens more
quickly.

~ November 11, 2014

Dear people who think you know more about what
gender I am than I do:

I know some doctors who can help you with that.
Just sayin'   Love, Stephanie

~ November 9, 2014

Love is the boomerang of life.

~ November 9, 2014

Doing my best to share kindness on the journey reveals truth that will not otherwise be known.

~ November 9, 2014

The journey is filled with stepping stones that are often disguised as obstacles.

~ November 9, 2014

I am never expected to be any better than I am capable of being. I am expected to become capable of being better, not necessarily from minute to minute or day to day, but as time goes by.

~ November 9, 2014

If someone isn't trying to knock me down, I'm not making enough noise.

~ November 7, 2014

stopped by Naps-R-Us on the way home and picked up a six-pack for the weekend.

~ November 6, 2014

I stand up and speak out not to those who disrespect love. I stand up and speak out to those who need to know that love is standing up and speaking out.

~ November 5, 2014

I am excited for the future because I know that the future belongs to people who are not willing to accept oppression, who are not indifferent to inequality, and who will not stop until we get there.

Dab says -

We needed to vote *en masse*, but we didn't. It is easy to become frustrated when the voices of oppression remain in power. We must never stop fighting.

~ November 4, 2014

So, I wake up in the morning and do the same thing I did today. Try to shine light into the darkness. Fight for equality. Work to replace injustice with justice. Demand my right to equal space in this world. Do my personal best to teach the purpose and value of love. Game isn't over. Game is on.

~ November 3, 2014

The only moral argument regarding laws protecting LGBT citizens is the need to treat all human beings equally under the law and with dignity & respect.

~ November 1, 2014

The thing that has changed in the LGBT rights movement is that more people than not are beginning to understand that this is a human rights issue. Children are taking their own lives because they can't imagine a life where they can be who they are and love who they love. People are suffering unimaginable horrors. Get with the program, people. Love is love. My authenticity comes from within me. We should be lifting up the people who are marginalized and oppressed, not putting them down. We must unite in the cause of worldwide humanity and unconditional love for all people. There is hope for the world, but hope is the gift of action. Stand on the side of love. Speak with the words of justice. Walk with the purpose of change. Live for the dream of freedom for everyone.

~ October 31, 2014

Halloween used to be a day that was less dangerous for me to take off my mask and reveal my true self. Let's create a world where everyone can feel safe in being who they truly are, all the time.

Dan Brennan, Davis Hammet, Joshua Longbottom and me at the Topeka Pride *Coming Out Costume Karaoke Party* at Serendipity.

~ October 27, 2014

I have been compared to the most horrible things on the planet. I guess it comes down to, do I want to respond to that or do I want to be effective at creating change?

The time has come when my adversaries have become my best witnesses. All I have to do is carry my head up and try to be kind.

~ October 25, 2014

In a world with so many people who seem to have a mission of teaching me "the truth", it is always a pleasure to spend time with a traveler on the journey of discovery.

~ October 25, 2014

I heard a person say that the voices of the young are not experienced enough to help solve the problems of the world and I wondered out loud how we could possibly solve the world's problems without the inclusion of all voices.

~ October 20, 2014

It is really quite simple at this point. If enough people who would like to see Kansas be a light for everyone, with values that include liberty and justice for everyone, if enough people with these hopes for our state get out and vote, we will win. If not, we will lose. Today is the first day for advance voting. What kind of Kansas would you like to see?

~ October 19, 2014

My hope for the world is directly tied to my willingness to give of myself for the benefit of all people who are marginalized and oppressed.

~ October 18, 2014

No one is less than.

~ October 17, 2014

Without compassion, even for those who have harmed me or harmed others, I have strayed from the path on which lies the answer. Unconditional love has no conditions.

~ October 17, 2014

Because I can take everything bad that happened and use it to try to create something good, it changes the pain and transforms the senselessness. I don't have to be angry. Instead of being held back for all that time, I was being prepared to carry the light and share the love. I believe it is a great gift - to be in a place where I can help people who need me - it is the greatest gift a person can receive.

~ October 15, 2014

I am not now, nor will I ever again be, silent in the face of oppression. If you try to bully me into silence, you will discover how loud my voice can be.

~ October 14, 2014

I think of God as a 7 billion-piece jigsaw puzzle and every person on the planet is one of those pieces.

~ October 11, 2014

I was sitting in the Colby (Kansas) Public Library in July 2011 talking about being transgender when one of the people in the audience asked me this question. Why would anyone tell people that they were transgender?

The questioner failed to understand the basic premise of their question. By asking that question they were saying that being transgender is something someone should hide. They were saying there is something wrong with being transgender. I lived in the darkness far too long. There are no windows in the closet. The sunlight can not reach in.

I have walked in the sunlight for quite some time now. My soul began to heal the moment I began to give myself permission to be me. My soul began to shine in the newly discovered light. My heartbeat sounded a different, honest and shameless truth. My downward gaze turned up and I began to look the world in the eye.

No, I won't hide myself from the world. The world has too much to offer and I have too much to offer the world.

~ October 10, 2014

There is great reason to hope for a better tomorrow and even greater reason to work for a better today. All of us helping all of us.

~ October 10, 2014

We are living history. Right now. These are the exact moments in time when our nation begins to truly come to an understanding that our relationships are valid. Our love is love. Our lives are not less than.

Yet, we have so far left to go and those who find their own worth in the oppression of other people will become even more daring and even more destructive in their pursuits.

There can be no going back to a day when we are not allowed to marry regardless of sexual orientation or gender identity. We must move forward to the day when no law in our great country serves to declare that anyone is a lesser human being.

We are most definitely living history. We have discovered the power of standing together and working not just for our own freedom but for the freedom of all people.

Truth is that there are no lesser human beings. Freedom is the day when no one is treated by our government as a lesser human being. We are on the path - so many miles yet to go - but we are on the path where these words will forever ring true - it is our right - it is our responsibility - with liberty and justice for all.

The Transgender Faith Tour traveled to Missouri and Oklahoma in October with presentations at the Joplin Diversity Fellowship, United Church of Norman UCC and Mayflower Congregational UCC (Oklahoma City).

~ October 9, 2014

There are still days when I wake up in the morning and see myself in the mirror of the dresser next to my bed, and I cry. They are tears of joy and wonderment that I am able to be my true self. It seemed so impossible for such a long time.

~ October 8, 2014

I think God's will is for people to stop using God's will as an excuse to marginalize other people.

~ October 7, 2014

If you boys don't start behaving, I'm going to go all ActivismIsLove on your bigoted backsides.

~ October 7, 2014

Today, I hope to hold open the door for someone else's hope. I hope to leave a kind mark on the world. I hope to reach out to those who misunderstand me. I hope to bring light into the darkness.

~ October 3, 2014

I did not enter the light to share darkness. I entered the light to share the light. To illuminate the path to the light. To hold open the door to the light. To offer the light to anyone who would choose it. Even those who kept me from the light. Because . . . the light.

~ September 27, 2014

They say that I am a bleeding-heart liberal. The intention is to frame the characteristic of having a heart that bleeds as a bad thing. I suppose the contrast to that would be having a heart that does not bleed. Like a heart of stone or something.

Too often, strength is measured in hardness. Too bad we don't measure strength in compassion. Hard is easy. Compassion take courage. Maybe some people can watch quietly as people and animals suffer in this world. I just don't happen to be one of them.

~ September 25, 2014

It was like wearing a pair of shoes that didn't fit. Painful, uncomfortable, awkward, incorrect. It made every single step I took more difficult (on trying to live as a man).

~ September 24, 2014

The choice is not between being a woman or being a man. The choice is between being authentic or play-acting. Letting my light shine or hiding in the darkness.

~ September 24, 2014

There is so much diversity in every aspect of our humanness. Why would that diversity not apply to sexual orientation and gender identity? How could it not apply?

So the question is not, "Why are there transgender people?"

The question is, "Why would there not be transgender people? "

Speaking at the Topeka
Center for Peace and
Justice - Turnaround
Tuesday LGBT Rally
at the State Capitol on
September 30.

photo credit: Dan Brennan

~ September 22, 2014

*It was simply not possible - exactly up and to the
moment that it became reality.*

~ September 17, 2014

For the least of these . . .
For the marginalized
For the oppressed
For the poor
For the hungry
For the tired
For the suffering
For the sick
For the imprisoned
For the stranger
For the downtrodden
For the heavy laden
For the weak
For them all

Chicago, September 12-14 with Jaymee Metzenthin

~ September 11, 2014

God obviously loves all of God's creation.

~ September 11, 2014

We move LGBT equality forward more quickly with consistent and open displays of radical love for all people, than by any other possible act.

~ September 10, 2014

Dream big, then get busy.

~ September 10, 2014

NFL, are you serious about domestic violence or not?

~ September 9, 2014

The advance of human dignity is inevitable. There will be only two remembrances. Those who helped move equality forward, and those who stood in the way. Which will you choose?

~ September 8, 2014

Topeka is Ready for a Different Tomorrow! Let's make that happen!

~ September 7, 2014

Q. What do you call it when more than 2000 people come together to celebrate diversity and stand up for the value of respect and dignity for all people?

A. 2014 Topeka Pride.

~ September 6, 2014

Happy 2014 TOPEKA PRIDE DAY!!! This is a day for truth, honesty, and authenticity. This is a day to celebrate who we are and who we can become. This is a day to celebrate those who stand beside us with courageous, unconditional love. No one is less than. This is a day to celebrate the FACT that we can walk together, hand in hand, using that courageous and unconditional love to create a world where no one is ever told that they are less than. Where no one ever believes they are less than. Where no one ever needs to come out because truth, honesty, and authenticity are always given the opportunity to shine in the light of love.

Topeka Pride, September 6th in the NOTO Arts District

photo credit: Dan Brennan

photo credit: Dan Brennan

~ August 24, 2014

I don't think believing that working for a living wage, treating all people with dignity and respect, wanting to end discrimination and poverty, having full access to affordable health care as defined between a patient and their doctor, and taking care of the planet are liberal values. These are middle-of-the-road, American values. Pay attention to who is saying these are not American values. Understand why they are saying that. Then vote them out of office.

~ August 23, 2014

Sometimes it is hard for me to wrap my mind around how much life has changed for me. The things I get to do these days absolutely astound me. Ain't nothing to do but ride the wave and see where it takes me. I'm kind of excited about that.

~ August 21, 2014

These people who are, like, down with this love thing, I don't know, it's like they're obsessed with it or something. Love your neighbor! Love your enemy! Love the sick! Love the poor! Love everybody! Can you imagine what might happen to this world if everyone acted like that?

~ August 20, 2014

They asked if you could go back and change one thing about your life, what would it be? I said I would learn to play hopscotch.

~ August 20, 2014

Civil rights ordinances protecting LGBT citizens are not controversial. Opposition to civil rights ordinances protecting LGBT citizens is controversial.

~ August 20, 2014

The power of the words I say is immeasurably influenced by the things I do.

~ August 18, 2014

When did back to school shopping start including the need to buy a new purse?

~ August 16, 2014

If I am not participating in the elimination of privilege, I am participating in privilege.

~ August 15, 2014

This will be my one & only about the death of Robin Williams.

A definition of privilege is that I believe something is not a problem because it is not a problem for me, personally. If I am not walking in your shoes, I do not know what it is like to walk in your shoes. I am, therefore, in no position to judge anything you do.

He was amazing. He will be missed. It is very sad. All that needs to be said.

~ August 15, 2014

This will be my one & only about the fallout from the shooting of Michael Brown in Ferguson, Missouri.

I hear many people asking the question, "Why would these people riot?"

I am wondering how many times we will ask that question without actually taking the time to find out the answer to it. Just sayin'

~ August 12, 2014

thinks it would be quite awesomesauce if we could all learn to not other each other

~ August 11, 2014

It has been a few years since the last time I was homeless. My pantry is filled with food. My heart is surrounded by people who love me. I think I will go with the idea that this is already an amazingly good day.

~ August 3, 2014

Anger is heavy. It makes it difficult to fly.

The Transgender Faith Tour was rocking in August! August 2nd presentation with Sue Gerth for a Catholic Women's group in Manhattan, August 3rd message at Unitarian Universalist Fellowship of Lawrence, August 10th message at Unitarian Universalist Fellowship of Topeka, August 17th for Sojourners Sunday School Class at First Baptist Church in Lawrence, and August 24th sermon at Central Congregational United Church of Christ in Topeka.

~ July 31, 2014

If you are giving up hope, come, spend an hour with me. I have enough for both of us. Hope is not the absence of fear. Hope is not separated from sadness. Hope is the understanding that there is a possibility for change. Hope is the gift of action. When I move my feet, my brain begins to believe it could maybe might happen. Hope walks hand in hand with love; side by side with gratitude; on the very same path as helpfulness to others.

If you are giving up hope, come, spend an hour with me. I have enough for both of us.

~ July 25, 2014

I live at the intersection of privileged and oppressed. Every step I take defines what is important to me.

~ July 22, 2014

The future belongs to all of us. Those who choose to treat others as lesser human beings will not prevail for we shall never cease our efforts to bring about a world where we are allowed to be who we are and love who we love.

TransKansas 2 - July 11-13
College Hill United Methodist Church in Wichita

July 23rd marked 8 years of embracing myself as Stephanie

Turning Circles

In the beginning, I knew. I was born female. I was born into a male body. I don't remember coming to this conclusion. I just knew. Things being what they were at the time, it never occurred to me that my situation was not truly mine, but a gift from a society that did not know, and did not want to know. Sadly, things are still not that much different.

In that "truth", I tried to play by the "rules", and the "roles". Every moment of my conscious existence was an exercise in futility. A battle between who I was, and who I thought I needed to be. At times, the battle lines seemed to be drawn between me, and the God who created me.

For 48 years, I struggled. The woman on the inside of me lay dormant, like a seed awaiting the springtime. Unable to grow in the absence of light. And the woman on the inside of me fought for her very life. Forced into the shadows. Desperately yearning for the light. The ever increasing torment leading to a new truth: Death would come, and the pain would finally end.

When things became so bad that I just couldn't take it anymore, I decided to pursue the woman of my soul. Enter the light. By the grace of God, through the love of many, in the moment that waited a lifetime, I was born. "God, bless your daughter, for the faith she has shown in you." These are the words I heard in the moment of my birth, as Stephanie took communion for the very first time.

In the last eight years, Stephanie has experienced life. She is no longer bound by the leashes of society. The tethers are cut by the need for the human soul to reach into the realm of truth, and the subsequent inability to ever return to a world of delusion and denial.

The truth. God's truth. I am a woman. I did not become a woman. I have always been a woman. I stopped pretending to be a man. When I stopped pretending to be someone else, I began to discover the woman who was always there.

Today, my soul reaches into the unknown with the innocence of a child, and the faith that comes from having seen the difference between fighting God, and surrendering to God. There is no tomorrow. Only today. And in this day, if I breathe the air of womanhood, and if I walk in the light, I am able to live in my soul. See it shine.

I have been blessed with a gift. The same precious gift that most 8-year-old girls have. It is mine. And I will keep it to myself until I find the one with whom I will share all of me.

In the meantime, I stand in the living room turning circles, twirling around like a little girl. For in my soul, this is who I am. After all, I have only been alive for a precious eight years.

~ July 6, 2014

Because I am transgender, my world revolves around oppression, advocacy, activism, prejudice, discrimination, and education with respect to transgender people.

Because I am white, Christian, middle-class, well-educated, AND transgender; I find in necessary to my well-being that my world revolve around oppression, advocacy, activism, prejudice, discrimination, and education with respect to all people.

~ July 5, 2014

Were I not transgender, I might have walked through life without gaining the understanding of privilege and oppression that I have today. It is an understanding that I consider to be one of my most prized possessions.

~ July 4, 2014

Third sentence in my Multicultural Practice class book - "Although equality has historically been denied to many, there is now a legal framework in place that guarantees protections from discrimination and equal treatment for all citizens."

Still in the same paragraph - " . . . lesbian, gay, bisexual, trans-gendered (LGBT) people . . . "

Oh, my, she said, with a wry smile on her face.

The fact that I am included in Ashley Laird's *Women's Mural* as part of the *Great Mural Wall of Topeka* is a remarkable and invaluable statement about how Kansas is changing. I don't know that I belong on this mural with these amazing women, but I am a woman, and it is most rewarding to know that there are women like Ashley who understand the importance of saying so.

~ July 3, 2014

Choosing to try to bring peace and love to the world is the first step.

~ July 2, 2014

Strength is not measured by how much power you hold. Strength is measured by how much you empower others. The truly strong lift people up. They don't keep people down. Open the door for someone's dreams.

~ July 1, 2014

I shall not be silent in the face of oppression.

~ June 30 2014

Everyone has to make their own choices, but I stopped shopping at Hobby Lobby a long time ago.

~ June 29, 2014

I am a piece of the puzzle. No more and no less valuable than any other piece. Without all of us, the puzzle can never be completed. Without each of us, the complete picture can not be seen. We are connected to each other and reliant on each other, and we can only achieve our purpose if we work together in harmony.

~ June 27, 2014

There is no greater privilege, no more meaningful right, no more important value, and no more courageous act than to be one's true, authentic self.

~ June 25, 2014

They are right. I would like to have special rights. I would like to have those special rights that heterosexual, cisgender people have, but LGBT people do not have. Now, if everyone has them, they won't be special rights anymore. Just human rights.

Sue & Stephanie New England Vacation, June 18-22

photos by Sue Gerth & Stephanie Mott

~ June 14, 2014

Hate knows no boundary other than love.

~ June 13, 2014

My hope is to display my humanity so authentically, to expose my heart in such a fashion, that it makes it exceedingly difficult for anyone to be able to see me as a lesser human being.

~ June 11, 2014

The most powerful tools in my equality toolkit are love, compassion, and kindness.

 On June 9th, well, there was this young woman who wanted to have a godmother and this somewhat older woman who didn't have a goddaughter and, well, they found each other.

~ June 5, 2014

If I change the world for only one person, I have changed the world.

~ June 1, 2014

I keep seeing articles about transgendered people written by ignoranted journalists.

~ June 1, 2014

Poverty is a form of violence.

~ May 28, 2014

I sow the seeds. God grows the garden. I am told to sow the seeds on good ground. But there is more. Some seeds help create the ground on which they fall. The seeds of bitterness and anger fall among thorns. The seeds of love and compassion fall on good ground. I don't always, even often, see the garden grow. But if I plant the seeds of love and compassion, I can be sure that the garden will grow. And someone I may never meet will gather their own seeds from the harvest.

~ May 27, 2014

Sometimes, it's best to play it close to the vest.
Sometimes, it's best to throw caution to the wind.
The trick, is knowing when to do which.

~ May 27, 2014

Every once in a while, you have to stir the soup.
When people see someone who isn't afraid to stir
the soup, they sometimes discover their own ability
to speak up.

~ May 26, 2014

Reducing your fellow human being to second-class
citizenship is the immoral act.

~ May 26, 2014

I do have a trans* agenda - to work for a world
where no trans* teenager believes suicide is a
necessary response to gender non-conformity.

~ May 25, 2014

How can I ask for your compassion if I am not
willing to give you mine? Your understanding?
Your acceptance? Your love?

~ May 25, 2014

A few more people spoke against the ordinance, than for it and I could see the reaction on City Council members faces while opponents were testifying and after those reactions, I knew it would pass,

~ May 24, 2014

As I remember those who have made the ultimate sacrifice for the freedoms I know, I will include those who have sacrificed their lives - both in terms of how they lived their lives and in terms of how they lost their lives - so that one day, LGBTQ children will not need to come out of the closet, because they will never have known the need to be in the closet.

~ May 21, 2014

The names you call me are the rungs on the ladder I shall use to climb from the hole in which you would have me live.

~ May 20, 2014

The City of Topeka has a Domestic Partnership Registry. One down. One to go.

~ May 20, 2014

Gender identity is now a protected class in City of Topeka employment. The City Manager is empowered to contract for health care benefits for same-sex partners of city employees.

 On May 20, 2014, the City of Topeka - City Council voted 5-3 to approve two ordinances. The first ordinance created a domestic partnership registry for the City of Topeka. The second ordinance added gender identity to the City's Non-Discrimination Policy for city employment and authorized the city manager to seek out health insurance benefits that would be inclusive for same-sex couples.

The passing of the ordinance was the culmination of many months of work by the Topeka Chapter of Equality Kansas with the extraordinary support of City Councilman Chad Manspeaker. The ordinances were hashed and re-hashed over three months by the City of Topeka Human Relations Commission, of which I am honored to be a member.

These efforts were also wonderfully supported by members of the Unitarian Universalist Fellowship of Topeka, Capital City NOW, Interweave Topeka, Equality House, and others.

The Topeka Chapter of Equality Kansas is dedicated to achieving the end of legalized discrimination against lesbian, gay, bisexual, and transgender citizens of Topeka and we will be working diligently to accomplish equality for LGBT citizens of Topeka in 2015. Come join us.

~ May 18, 2014

The seed of compassion was planted in my heart. For that, I can take no credit. In that, I am challenged to bring that seed to life through acts of compassion. A seed lies dormant until it begins to grow.

The seed of compassion grows in the warmth and light of love, freely received and freely given. Compassion, like love and gratitude, is not just a feeling. For compassion to grow, it must be placed into action. Then, compassion grows quickly in the sunlight of love, and my heart grows too.

One day, I begin to understand the gifts and responsibilities that come with holding the seed of compassion in my heart, because this gift has the remarkable ability to plant itself in the hearts of others. New seeds take flight on the wings of love and the winds that are stirred by acts of kindness.

Compassion is contagious. Spread the love.

~ May 15, 2014

Because I am an advocate for people who are transgender; I am also an advocate for the homeless; an advocate against suicide; an advocate for fair housing; an advocate for equal employment opportunity; an advocate against poverty; an advocate for access to health care; an advocate for fair treatment by law enforcement; an advocate for fair treatment for people who are incarcerated; an advocate for immigration rights; an advocate for HIV/AIDS awareness, research, and services; an advocate for education; an advocate for fair borrowing practices; an advocate against racism, sexism, ableism, and classism; and more.

May 17, 2014 was graduation day. I am distinctly honored to have achieved a Bachelor of Social Work degree from Washburn University.

~ May 10, 2014

I don't understand this "allow" marriage equality idea. Equality is endowed. Humankind can not allow equality. We can only cease to deny it. And we do not cease to deny equality until we devote ourselves to putting an end to inequality.

~ May 2, 2014

Because I know what it feels like to be judged, I will try to not judge others. Because I know what it feels like to be afraid, I will work to help others find courage. Because I know what it feels like to be excluded, I will seek to become more inclusive. Because I know what it feels like to be alone, I will try to be there when someone needs me.

~ May 2, 2014

I want to be the light that shines into your closet when you finally decide to open the door.

~ May 1, 2014

When someone fights for some "right" to discriminate, they have made the only argument required to prove the need for laws to protect from discrimination.

~ April 30, 2014

We are all just doing the best we can to make the world a better place. Each of us helping all of us.

~ April 28, 2014

The limits of my capacity to change the world are determined by my willingness to try, my desire to take the high road, and by putting into place the corresponding action.

~ April 27, 2014

I must own my responsibility to eliminate my privilege or own the truth that I think it is acceptable. I can't have it both ways.

~ April 26, 2014

As many times as I am amazed by some of the harmful things people do, I am amazed 10 times over by some of the wonderful things people do.

~ April 25, 2014

So, that we can change the world thing? I meant that.

~ April 25, 2014

I've decided that working to create change is better for my soul than complaining. I've decided that working to create change is better for my soul than remaining silent. I've made those two decisions every morning for the last six years.

~ April 25, 2014

You know it's going to be a good day when your first conversation of the day includes coming out as trans*.

~ April 24, 2014

Love works miracles.

~ April 21, 2014

Equality is waiting for enough people to say we can't wait any longer. What are you saying?

~ April 20, 2014

is thinking that since I am only going to make 77 cents on the dollar, my tuition should only be 77 cents on the dollar. And my books.

~ April 20, 2014

I am not afraid of what will happen if I spread my wings. I am afraid of what will happen if I don't.

~ April 18, 2014

Today I will work on forgiveness, for it is difficult for my soul to fly on the wings of resentment, and I have come to appreciate those moments in which my soul is able to fly.

On April 12th, at the year-end banquet for the Washburn Social Work Student Association, I was honored to receive the Donna Love Award for outstanding social work student for 2014.

Donna Love, a 1943 Washburn University graduate, headed efforts that directly resulted in what we know today as the social work department at Washburn University. She not only led the pathway to the BSW program, but also developed a Masters in Social Work degree that was approved by the Council on Social Work Education in 1993.

~ April 16, 2014

When I open myself up to the possibilities of the universe, the possibilities of the universe open up to me.

~ April 16, 2014

Subjecting an entire class of human beings to second-class status is not the free expression of an idea. It is pure and horrifying bigotry. We should not condemn those who speak up against bigotry. We should celebrate them. And join them.

~ April 15, 2014

I am asked to use this day to bring light into the world, to sow the seeds of love and compassion, to lift up the downtrodden, and to offer hope to those who have lost hope. All things are possible when you walk in the light of love.

~ April 14, 2014

The path to enlightenment is not illuminated by telling someone what they should be doing, but by allowing them to see the value of doing something for others.

~ April 13, 2014

It was as if someone opened the door through which the nightmare was not allowed to follow. As if every moment, up to that moment, was some sort of horrible existence, and in that moment, life began.

~ April 13, 2014

The greatest privilege a person can have in this world is to wake up in the morning knowing that you have the opportunity to make a difference in the life of someone who is oppressed.

On April 12th, K-STEP was honored to award the *Jane Newman Pioneer Award* to Sandra Meade, the *Paula Keiser For the Kids award* to Sue Gerth and the *K-STEP Ally Award* to Thomas Witt. The K-STEP Awards recognize individuals and organizations for meritorious effort in achieving transgender education, awareness, and equality.

photo - L-R - Sandra Meade, Sue Gerth, Stephanie Mott, Mary Haller, and Thomas Witt.

~ April 10, 2014

The smile on my face might be the light someone needs to see today. The kindness of my words might be the thing that helps someone carry on.

~ April 8, 2014

That awkward moment when you learn enough about someone that all the stuff they said, that had you scratching your head, suddenly makes a lot more sense.

~ April 6, 2014

I only danced one dance. But it was a very nice dance. I got to be vulnerable in a safe space. Unsure of how to be led, as opposed to lead.

But what I saw took me back to a day not quite four years ago, when I presented at my first national transgender conference. We had a dinner on Saturday evening, and there were about 100 people in the room, most of us transgender. No one needed to hide their true self. Everyone able to just be, and be free. No looking over the shoulder to see who was watching. No pretense of presenting some asinine version of who you are supposed to be. Just be. And be free. Natural. Correct. True.

Tonight, what I saw were young people being able to do what they do best. Be alive and be unencumbered by the fabricated and false expectations of a world that far-too-often gathers evidence from fear and ignorance.

And what I saw was joy. The kind of joy that can only come from the freedom of self. The kind of joy we deny our children when we attempt to create them, rather than to enable them to create themselves. What I saw contained no such denial. No need for it. No place for it.

I only danced one dance. But it was a very nice dance. I got to be vulnerable in a safe space. Unsure of how to be led, as opposed to lead.

~ April 3, 2014

The condensed history of the world.

Haters gonna hate.
Lovers gonna love.
Love wins.

~ The End ~

~ April 2, 2014

I have a responsibility to humanity to color outside the lines.

~ March 31, 2014

A question I get from time to time: Why would you tell someone that you are transgender?

The answer (in the form of a question): Why would I not?

~ March 30, 2014

I am all genders. I cover the spectrum of orientations. I am every belief system and every ethnicity. Every race and every ability. I am limited by our infinite need to place people in boxes. I strive to move beyond my fears and experience life with open eyes, an open heart, and an open mind. I am limited by my unwillingness to embrace the people who have intimate knowledge of the parts of me I have yet to discover; I have yet to embrace. My soul is set free by my unwillingness to be defined, or to define others, by such limitations. Live the journey.

~ March 29, 2014

It is my place as a human being to lift up those who have been oppressed, and to reach out to those who have been left behind. This place does not preclude the idea of standing up to bigotry. It requires it.

~ March 28, 2014

You know you're making a difference when you are accused of pushing the 'queer' agenda and being called out by name.

~ March 27, 2014

When we see how today's youth embraces an understanding of gender that does not align with the gender binary, we should see them as our teachers, instead of our students. This is what it looks like when you allow it to be natural; when you allow it to be what it truly is.

 In 2007, Marion Shorman invited me into her home to recover from hip surgery. I had no idea that she was about to become my second mom, and that I was about to become her daughter, the daughter I believed I would never get to be. Yay!

~ March 24, 2014

believes that everyone is worthy of love.

~ March 24, 2014

I could condemn those who condemn me, if I wanted to be like them. But then, I have to ask myself: How will that make things better? What am I trying to accomplish? Feel good about striking back, or change the world? I choose change the world.

~ March 21, 2014

If we're going to change the world, it's going to be through love.

~ March 20, 2014

Kansas Statewide Transgender Education Project continues to ask for responses to the news of Fred Phelps' death to be based in dignity and respect. We, as gender non-conforming people; as LGBT people, friends, families, and allies; are worthy of dignity and respect. We earn that right by our existence. We keep that right by our actions.

~ March 16, 2014

Abandon all forms of hate and carry the torch of love. True courage is the ability to respond not in kind, but with kindness. Lift up the light of love. Our hope for a better tomorrow depends on love. Ask, and it shall be given. Seek, and you shall find. It is the hour to shine, or sink into the trap. Love endures all things. Choose love.

~ March 14, 2014

It is a great fine day to kick some hate-butt.

~ March 11, 2014

The path to a better world is built on the steps we take to help each other.

~ March 10, 2014

woke up from a dream that she adopted a baby girl; is feeling some amazingly beautiful feelings.

~ March 4, 2014

If I had been a man, there would have been no need for me to live as a woman. The reason I couldn't be a man is because that's not who I was.

~ March 4, 2014

I have claimed my right to be openly, unashamedly me.

~ March 1, 2014

It's called acceptance. Not exceptance.

~ February 27, 2014

Failing to embrace diversity is like choosing to see a black and white rainbow.

~ February 21, 2014

How does one rightly go about being a woman? After all, I spent many years trying to figure out how one rightly goes about being a man – to no avail, I might add. Thus, seven years ago I began the process of discovering, uncovering, and recovering the woman of my soul.

February 15, 2014 - Womyn Rising Conference

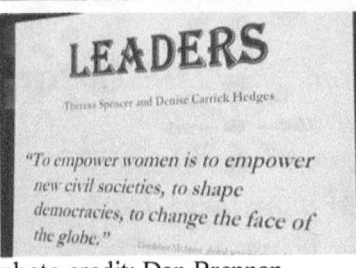

photo credit: Dan Brennan

~ February 21, 2014

My gift to the world today shall be my true authentic self.

~ February 18, 2014

I am not a second-class citizen. It is time to take a stand.

~ February 12, 2014

It is my hope to expose my humanity to the point that you can not see me as a lesser human being.

~ February 4, 2014

I have tasted the nectar of truth. I shall never again dine in the land of pretend.

~ January 31, 2014

I have photographs of me from when I used to live as a man and when you compare them to photographs of me today, beyond the physical transition, there is a spiritual transition. It is evidenced by the lack of a light in my eyes before, and the undeniable presence of a light in my eyes today.

~ January 30, 2014

Love wins. Whenever prejudice and discrimination are met with love, love wins. When any human being chooses love over hate, love wins. When any heart allows love to be its guide, love wins. Confuse not the battle for the war. Love wins.

~ January 29, 2014

is wondering where the road is leading her, but certain that she has been prepared for the journey.

~ January 26, 2014

I am at peace with the universe. That does not mean that I like everything. There are many things in this world that I find reprehensible. It means that I understand, at least for the moment, my place in trying to take that which is reprehensible, to the best of my ability, and replace it with love.

 Mr. Kitty has been my companion for about eight years, now. He has taken up residence on my piano bench and he does not like it when I put him down. He glares at me from across the room until I dutifully evacuate my presence from his place of rest and relaxation. Other than that, he's perfect.

~ January 24, 2014

I think it's cool that I can type Stephanie Mott's
Uterus into Google and this is what comes up.

News for stephanie mott's uterus

Trans-Uterus
Huffington Post - 3 days ago
Complicating the simple is a human talent. You
might think that the human endeavor should be
fraught with efforts to simplify the complicated,

~ January 24, 2014

What I failed to understand was that making the
world better for me, meant working to make to
world better for others.

~ January 22, 2014

is having one of those days where there are two
sets of footsteps in the sand.

~ January 17, 2014

Create space in your world to allow others to talk
about the things they need to talk about. There is

no greater compliment of humanity than to have someone trust you enough to share their secrets.

~ January 13, 2014

I didn't decide to become an activist. I just decided that I needed to do something about injustice. That activist thing just kind of happened after that.

~ January 12, 2014

The song in my heart is alive today. No one should have a problem with that.

~ January 10, 2014

The sparkle in my eyes is the reflection of the light in which I choose to live today.

2014 was a year that saw me embrace my voice and record and publicly post videos of some of my songs on YouTube. It turns out that authenticity has to be 24/7 or it's not really authenticity.

~ January 9, 2014

At the end of the day, there are two questions I need to ask myself.

1. Have been true to myself? Being true to myself includes being true to my identity, true to my values, and true to my relationship with the world.

2. What can I do tomorrow to do that better? Because I am a work in progress, never aiming to become anything, except better.

~ January 6, 2014

Sometimes, I see something, and I kind of pause for a second, and I get that look of awesome wonder on my face, and I am reminded of the many miracles that are part of my life every day.

What would happen if a person saw things that way more often? What would happen?

~ January 4, 2014

I became a woman in the sense that a girl becomes a woman. Not in the sense that a man becomes a woman.

~ January 3, 2014

If I want my life to change, I need to do the things that change my life.

Thank you for allowing me to share some of my thoughts and some of the stops from my 57th year on the planet. I hope it has been enjoyable for you.

I have been so amazingly fortunate to have experienced the amazing love of many friends along my journey. Anything I accomplish happens in the light of your love.

The struggles that face many people who are transgender are unbelievably horrifying. It is not by anger and hate that we change this unfortunate truth. It is by love.

I am forever grateful to the many people in my life who have gifted me with the understanding that love conquers all.

This collection of my thoughts, experiences, and photographs is dedicated to those who would make this a better world for all humankind.

Peace, Blessings & Joy! (God's PB&J)

Stephanie